ESKATOS
&
THE STRETCHED NECKS OF STILLNESS

ESKATOS & THE STRETCHED NECKS OF STILLNESS

Mats Söderlund

Translated from the Swedish by Olivia Olsen

RESTLESS BOOKS
NEW YORK · AMHERST

First published as *Eskatos, tystnaden tillhör inte oss* by Albert Bonniers Förlag, Stockholm, 2023, and *Stillhetens sträckta halsar* by Albert Bonniers Förlag, Stockholm, 2002

First Restless Books paperback edition February 2026

Paperback ISBN: 9781632064158

Library of Congress Control Number: 2025942577

The cost of this translation was supported by a subsidy from the Swedish Arts Council, gratefully acknowledged.

SWEDISH
ARTSCOUNCIL

Cover illustration and design by Sarah Schulte
Text design and typesetting by Tetragon, London

The authorised representative in the EEA is eucomply OÜ, Pärnu mnt 139b–14, 11317 Tallinn, Estonia
(email: hello@eucompliancepartner.com / phone: +33757690241)

Printed in the United States

10 9 8 7 6 5 4 3 2 1

RESTLESS BOOKS
NEW YORK • AMHERST

restlessbooks.org

the living trees are a part of the dead trees
the dead trees are a part of the living trees
of these waves songs would be sung

WERNER ASPENSTRÖM

Contents

A Note on What You Hold in Your Hands

Mats Söderlund's *The Stretched Necks of Stillness*, rendered into English with what my bilingual friends tell me is "quiet precision" by Olivia Olsen, is, for me, one of those rare poetic achievements that thrums with both spiritual resonance and contemporary urgency. The second of two works collected in this volume, *Stillness* is a long-form meditation on life, death, and landscape, consisting of 186 stanzas—each deceptively simple, but collectively forming a dense and luminous weave, a sort of mycelial complex. In shifting rhythms, subtle emotive interiorities, and addresses—to the moss-and-lichen-matted landscape, to the beloved, the dead, the light, the reader—Söderlund goes about erasing any membrane between the material world and felt experience. Instead of a collection of lyric moments, the book takes place as one extended breath stretching across grief, memory, and ecological awareness.

Frankly, for me *The Stretched Necks of Stillness* has near-mythic status. I first saw the manuscript as one of twenty or so submitted at the end of a translation seminar I was teaching at Brown University. The title alone evokes tenuous stalks of moss reaching lightward. The work's striking originality, formal discipline, and emotional power, as well as the way it so effectively synthesizes the ecological and the personal, bowled me over. Of course, I immediately met with the translator, Olivia Olsen, and encouraged her to try to publish it. Over the years, I also sent it out to editors myself. The Center for the Art of Translation, characteristically alert to signal works brought into English, featured a section of the translation. But otherwise, no publisher committed to the work of a poet—unknown in the US—who writes obsessively about the northern Swedish landscape with such tenderness and clarity. That is, no publisher until savvy poet-translator Ilan Stavans, with his long antennae and appetite for urgent international literature, lassoed the manuscript for Restless Books.

For fifteen years, I had carried my dog-eared manuscript of Olsen's translation. In three different houses, I kept it by my desk like a holy relic. It is one of the few books that I would dare compare to Inger Christensen's magisterial *Alphabet*. My personal attachment speaks to the poem's lasting emotional depth. Its lyric voice stays intimate without being confessional. A line such as "gray and whitegleaming/ fingers reaching through moss" exemplifies Söderlund's signature style: poised between the corporeal and the ephemeral, hinting at the fragile interconnectivity between all living things. *Stillness* was a primary influence on my own book *Twice Alive*.

I think you'll find that Söderlund's poetry erases the border between an external world and inner feeling. Söderlund doesn't merely describe the moss-matted forests or the skeletal trees of the north—he lets them speak, mourn, and persist in a language of syntactical openness. The material world becomes a repository for memory and a witness to human grief. The landscape is not a backdrop but an actor in the drama of loss and persistence. In this sense, his work operates on a nearly animistic plane, one in which trees and rocks carry the same emotional weight as human voices. This ecological attunement marks one of the most compelling dimensions of his poetry.

Twenty years after the publication of *Stillness*, Söderlund wrote a book-length *cri de cœur* companion poem titled *Eskatos* (from the Greek meaning "last" or "utmost," the root of *eschatology*, the concern for final things; end times). It opens with the fierce imperative "Sing rage and collapse," echoing Homer's "Sing, goddess, of Achilles' wrath." But where Homer invokes Calliope, the muse of epic poetry, Söderlund's apostrophe is addressed to Mnemosyne, the goddess of memory—anchoring apocalypse not in heroism, but in remembrance. Instead of Agamemnon, Söderlund alludes to Armageddon: an illuminated night of world-ending that unfolds across shifting perspectives—I, it, they, we—reflecting a collective responsibility. In Olsen's translation, the references to ecological devastation are threaded with occasional rhymes that glint like faint traces of hope in a depleted world. In this poem-epic, "last things" are recollected, lamented, and, at least in memory, briefly rekindled.

Here, as in *Stillness*, Söderlund's landscapes are not passive beauties but endangered terrains. His imagery often foregrounds the vulnerability of ecosystems, subtly implicating human beings in their degradation. In a literary climate increasingly attentive to the Anthropocene, *Eskatos & the Stretched Necks of Stillness* stands out not for its polemic, but for its lyrical interrogation of complicity. It asks not only how we grieve for each other, but how we might grieve for vanishing environments, and whether poetry itself can become a form of ecological witness. What makes this volume ultimately indispensable is its refusal to separate existential, emotional, and ecological inquiries. In doing so, it transcends the poetic fashions of our moment and reclaims poetry as a space for profound ethical and interior engagement. It is not a book that shouts—it listens. It listens to the slow murmur of forests, to the echoes of the dead, and to the rhythms of the living trying to make sense of absence. For those willing to enter its stillness, it offers not only beauty, but revelation.

FORREST GANDER
July 2025

A Note from the Translator

I first came across Mats Söderlund's work almost twenty years ago, in the form of a few lines cited in a review of his fifth book of poetry, *Stillhetens sträckta halsar* (2002). I was transported: I felt at once the dense, slightly metallic scent of wet moss and looked down to see copper-colored marsh water seep over my rubber boots.

To the reader, Söderlund's landscape is immediately recognizable. He moves through the peat-rich wetlands and subalpine forests of the northern Swedish interior, a world he knows intimately. He names the smallest shrub and places it with precision in its ecosystem; he captures the specific shades of red in the grasses of a mire, the distinctive, mechanical whir of a diving common snipe (*Gallinago gallinago*), the star shapes made by lichen on a rock face, the scent of sun-warmed pine. He references traditional agricultural methods adapted to a land of short summers with endless daylight and, with as much familiarity, names the byproducts of the industrial processes that have taken their place, in which rivers become hydropower dams and forests, paper pulp.

It is this clarity, this deep familiarity, that first drew me to translate Söderlund. For Swedish readers who know these tableaux as intimately as he does, his poems will evoke, as they did for me, something familiar—a scent, a memory.

How to render Söderlund's terrain in all its faithfulness while making it readable in a new, American context?

Take, for example, *Salix glauca* (Swedish: *ripvide*), a small, subarctic shrub with downy gray-green leaves. In English, the common name—gray willow or glaucous willow—could easily be mistaken for any number of other willow species, most of which conjure an entirely different landscape. Swedish readers will recognize other species, such as signal crayfish, pond slider, and contorta pine, as invasive; these, and several others that Söderlund lists in *Eskatos, the silence does not belong to us*, are native to North America and might, for an ecologically literate American reader, invite a very different connotation. Those connotations aside, it has been a balancing act to retain Söderlund's exactness, in which every species is given its name, while remaining true to his style, which is rhythmic, sound-driven, and concise.

There are a few quirks of the Swedish language that help shape the meter and density of Söderlund's lines. One is its extensive use of compound words. Almost all Swedish common names of species, for example, are compounds. In *Eskatos*, a recitation of owl species, "jorduggla hökuggla/pärluggla slaguggla kattuggla," creates a regular, falling rhythm; each name begins with a stressed syllable followed by a secondary stress typical of Swedish compound words. A literal translation, "earthowl hawkowl/pearlowl strikeowl catowl," could convey that rhythm, as well as the evocative quality of the Swedish. But these are real species in danger of extinction; they deserve to be correctly named and remembered. Thus, in my final translation, they are short-eared owl, northern hawk owl, boreal owl, Ural owl, and tawny owl.

Compounds also provide a useful construction for neologisms, something Söderlund makes particular use of in *The Stretched Necks of Stillness*. As a result of their prevalence, these do not call attention to themselves the way they would in English. Nonetheless, I frequently chose to preserve them as an integral part of Söderlund's style, particularly as a means to build urgency in the later stanzas.

Another quirk of Swedish is its more sparing use of articles. Where English uses the definite article, "the," Swedish attaches a suffix to the noun, altering both its cadence and its visual compactness. Similarly, while English often employs possessive constructions with "of," Swedish predominantly uses the "-s" genitive (consider the difference between "the voices of the dead" and "the dead's voices"). Söderlund will use this construction to alter an image and create forward movement, whereas changing the order of the nouns reverses that movement.

This was a particular challenge with *Stillness*, a poem composed as a single sentence that builds phrase upon phrase to maintain a syntactic momentum across 186 stanzas. Söderlund achieves this, in part, through the semantic flexibility of words like "som," which—depending on its placement in a line—can shift from a relative pronoun (that) to a subjunction (as) to a prepositional comparison (like). Often, I have simply had to choose, abandoning ambiguity for the sake of clarity.

The strict, five-line form of *Stillness* encloses a world that is boundless, porous, and shifting. It speaks to the presence in our lives of the dead and memory, the cyclical nature of life, of every organism's—plant, animal, fungi—inextricable belonging to every other. The particulars of the landscape through which Söderlund moves suggest something eternal;

they are what remains after death, and they embody death, becoming a place of solace for the griever. The speaker loses themself in a pathless wild, which serves both as an escape and a repository of memories.

In *Eskatos*, the same terrain—and Söderlund's enumeration of species within it—has become a litany of losses. Here, grief is not individual, but a collective anguish for the unraveling cycle of life and death that once defined us. The speaker's movements over the land are characterized by an awareness not of the endless, teeming presence found within the previous work, but of absence: species lost, populations thinned, patterns interrupted, rifts opened in the fabric of the ecosystem. The land loses its role as a repository of memory, loses its very language. As in *Stillness*, the speaker's will moves outward—away, gone—but the means of escape have closed. The wish to be gone is now a wish for oblivion, a refusal to exist.

Time is a curious thing. *Eskatos*, published in Sweden in 2023, is Söderlund's latest work, and marks the second time I have translated his poetry. *Stillness* was written more than twenty years ago and translated not long after. I am the same age now as the poet was when he wrote *Stillness*, and twice the age I was when I translated it. The steady news of extreme weather, wildfires, floods, and shrinking glaciers paints a future that is already here. *Eskatos* makes clear that the world we knew is gone, and our hope, if there is such a thing, will have to change shape. The book ends, nonetheless, in solace—the quiet comfort that, after this, something else will come.

OLIVIA OLSEN
Stockholm, February 2025

ESKATOS,
THE SILENCE
DOES NOT
BELONG
TO US

As we sow so shall we fall
as we fall so shall we lie
the crops have failed
we have no more to give
the dry earth.

Sing rage and collapse
our freedom burns
like the mire's yellow hay
to this we will never
return

sing our thoughtless grief
out where the sedge is cut and bound
where the scythe sweeps us down

sing our bodies' longing
where we learned to bear loss
in the wet meadows
bogmoss and sundew their
murmuring swarms of mosquitoes

sing Surtr the black
where smoke halts the eye
over miles of horizon
and the mirelands
burn

sing eskatos flames
where the range grows blue
against blackening skies
and the mountain
burns

sing Armageddon where dell
and aedna
burn

sing Sila where the permafrost
and national parks
rainforests
coral reefs

sing Pachacuti
where the ice sheets burn

where city parks burn
and cemeteries

sing where parking lots
and suburbs

sing where villages burn

sing djinns
that torch the cities
and overthrow the emperor

sing sighs of the Demiurge
where decay makes haste
and we lay us down
together

sing rotting trees
sing rotting ground
mushrooms and berries
birds that rot
like lovers
we fall and we rot
we make ourselves unfit to eat
together

make ourselves repulsive poisonous
infect the earth
and dream apocalypse

dream acharit hayamim
ragnarök and the sixth extinction

dream Kalki, Shiva, Gog and Magog
dream Azrael, dream Iblis
rotting and burning

dream galley ships and
endless credit

dream Vigrid and Molok
among the best
and the worst

the indifferent that rot
and those that burn

smoke is the smoke of our days

while longhorn beetles
and gleaming scarabs
breed in the thistle's
dusty brushes
out on the fallow field
we lie down
between roots and moon
and rot and burn
together

drunk on the wellspring's scents
horsetails and alder
together

drunk on acid rain and forest death
on blacklisted lakes and plastic seas

drunk in the gully's
merciful murmur
ozone hole out and away
together

gone

together

in the mosses on the mire
in the compost by the church
the recycling stations and
secondhand
stores overgrown
with mold and scum

muskrat knotweed swamplantern

rivers without water
silkweed signal-crayfish

the scythe that sweeps and
gathers us

hogsbane golpar

painted over children's
drawings in plastic bags

pondslider
raccoondog

contorta

how I want
and the rubber boots
under the coveralls at the back door
a young person's hunger and
love

to this we will never return
we have been misled

we are no longer here

not even the dead
remember us now

fair enough

fair if no one
wakes us

sing rage

sing grief
sing despair

and last curses

for those laid bare
and those forgotten all
                                        our wanting
out
                          gone.

See four horsemen charge
over the oat field see
the smoking pines
stain the sunset
distant but up close

see the desperate face
to face
their whitened knuckles
on our arms

see the frost crack
the backstreets
and a nightfall silent
on our ancient dread

see the asphalt split
like blunt force
on skin or
lips in sunlight

see time arch
its foaming body
from hope to hopelessness
gallop along earth's
stretch marks

see teeth rattle on public transit
buses thump over speed bumps
passengers bellow like cattle
in the stockyards

see us weave our fingers in grief and
love hound us round the bonfire
the debris of our longing

see the flames grow inside us
see fire ravage the village green
and the sky blush like old classmates
from junior high
no sooner forgotten
and faded

and I too want to fade

I turn away
struggle to not have to struggle

where I go you cannot follow.

*

There were in the beginning only voices
winding in the dark earth underground

ferried through moldering humus
they were us before we knew better

                    they rose through
wordless layers
sought a hold for the fire
                    the language we carried.

Mnemosyne goddess of memory
never grow sick of singing me

your silence walks at my heels
head held high and lost
as never
before

scents come in close
a warm wooded hill

sing sweat and wine
sing all that remains

tell me follow me
play me again and again

drink me

write me.

Am I among those calling
who do not see nor hear
am I a voice among voices
a song from underground
where pines and grasses
already grow high
above our scalps with
aeolian harps their ringing
all-hearing chorus
the musicians' stares
stretch speechless
over the marshes
and the strings quiver
in the dusk that
sounds inside us.

I swam under the humus
gasping for breath
like a carp
in the garden pond's
sludge

sing Mnemosyne
of Vigrid
and the miles
of shaggy heather

sing the days
of thirst and wanting
sing your return

and my breath
in the wavy hairgrass.

I long for light through earth and ice
a lust on nights as slick as spears
now all the lovers' ballads wake
and the soul is a wellspring the
body a blinding spark all the world's
rising fires foliage alight
burning horizons burning
forests and cities blind
bridges grasping at their supports
over the river the city's breath vibrates
like a vision
coughing loneliness in the
lit-up night.

Life and almost life in nightmare glow
in ditches stagnant and fire-

bellied toads their mating calls
the wellsprings' stream
do they babble
are we silent
and do we grieve those still alive
a bed of coals

the cars that swarm
the interstate's
and amphibians'

singing throats.

Sing us Mnemosyne
we are afraid of everything

that the world will end
and not begin again

that we are hunted without knowing
what is hunting us

that it will catch up to us
and the forest fail us then

those we have lost
bear witness to the end

the sawed-off willows in
the churchyard

rear up like mythic beasts
out of the mist

mount up—mount up
the final night unfolds.

In grief in grace and mercy
they rise up like flames

out of the scrub burning everything
grows here but voiceless

the words and songs fall silent
the woods embrace my steps

time engraved in the outcrop
with red bows and arrows
of hunger

but here they cannot reach
                    flight
                                I fight.

The tiny Apollo
Parnassius Mnemosyne

your memory is my memory

creator of meaning of words of forgetting
you fluttered a time over the hay meadows

the wings the wings

they wane
they wane

the scythe and rake

monochrome snaps in a
scattered album

out   gone.

Still in dream of a place without us
I walk across the peat
the rugs of braided roots

deaf and dumb and for miles and miles
you sway beside my mouth
water pulsates in our wake

gnats sting my groin mosquitoes
nestle at my throat
the path fades into grasses

close our eyes and sink
tell us in silence to one another.

To this I will never return
the abandoned dairy
the shuttered workshop
a smell of oil and animal skins
blue coveralls and rubber boots
hantavirus in the walls
I am lost and do not want
to find my way back.

Teach me to believe the miracle
teach me to repeat the lie
my body's longing
and waves of lust
tongues of horror
the furs crawl with maggots
and the rubber boots crack
I am lost
and do not want to find my way back.

The nylon line draws tight into the murk
and quivers when the spinner hooks
the stream
like all our longing
a clear voice in shadow and gleam
that once sang in my bones
twigs and leaves drift on the surface
memories laid over memories
those quietly absent who
vanish with us where the river
slows in the bend.

The clear-cut behind me
the sun in my eyes

blackflies at my nostrils
fish slime on my fingers

I did not know all this
was also fleeting

and just as photographs have not preserved
the sound of the snipe's

vibrating wings
as it dove over the marsh

it cannot be remembered
back.

Grieving in the stars
of sunwarmed bogmoss
steaming paper-pulp

in a warm bed of heather and drunk
on wild rosemary we roll
over on our backs

a cluster of white blossoms
at the tip of each branch
leathery leaves and
scented oils

the place gapes silent in the gloom
but a memory of the Mass
sounds in the treetop organs
and in the grasses' requiem.

I walk through the place
where you danced sapling

reaping moments branches
pineleaves mayflies

backward through the daylight
lost in smoke in voices

that soon the rain
the dark the trees the bark

like the word alone soon
and plows in the earth

that all the light we lost
will shine again

and spring sowing

soon.

The fritillary's last wingbeats
we saw without pausing
we hurried on
misled
not by beauty
but time and idleness
heard the darkness grow
and wished
we had taken our time with
those who left
that we had not seen them as given
that we had saved the scents
of meadowsweet and haymaking.

No matter how high the birches strain
the light recedes at last and the summer evening closes

the nightwatch has not yet come

and in between shifts
the woods a moment are still

I kneel down
by the garden pond

the dirty surface patiently
urging

water lilies encircle the birdsong
treecreeper robin and wren
murmur in expectation

I take in the teeming
ecosystem
in a single breath

everyone that has ever
been close to me.

The garden warbler is talking nonsense
it won't survive
nothing will survive
all things will grow
all things renew
the waves of grain
the toils of spring
it's over now
it starts again
all things will climb
out of themselves
breathe through the black
earth
all things will meet and beat and bleed
such is time
all things die
all things become new
you will die
and I with you.

Listening to the breaths of night in
the chimney long after the fire
has died ashes emptied the house
laid to rest long after the walls
have crumbled and the grass climbed in
long after the bricks have scattered
long after the dream has faded
the wind keeps whispering

wake wake wake

life life life.

Clutching at the line breaks

even they must cease

be silent without pause.

* *

Skrerkkkekekee
wrlh wrlh
teeth in warm wet rubberbloom
spitting sanders and hardware stores
screws and scrap and stone
hate electric scooters and innovative solutions
to what
krlsg krlsg
steel on steel on plastic synthetics
black gaskets brake discs
out of death rise highrises
out of dying the strip malls swell
out of vanishing bodies all the earth's
radiance
ice and glass and steel
sharpened polished refined
we gather in small spaces
we gnaw each other's throats
flesh and grass grass and flesh
gas clouds form medial
incarnations of: desperate searching
pay more pay better, receive in return:

desperate searching
ghrrrrrrrlll
rare earth packed into boxes with copper thread
our shattered civilization all we eat
are pieces of ourselves
the hunger never ends we are hunger
civilization is hunger
language itself is hunger hunger itself is
paint and white canvases on lonely easels along the
seaside
the factory directors line up with their scythes
grindstones round our necks we are the directors
hate Brazilian meat for real it should be il-
legal here
hate that no one draws the line between want and need
know only that I want to go on living
and that the common snipe
klrk klrk klrk
let me into DOLLAR STORE
gather outside BEST BUY
see you by HOME DEPOT
meet up outside WALMART
burn the e-scooters at TARGET
the PWCs
the ATVs
the SUVs
the jeans all the jeans I hate jeans jeans jeans jeans
up to fucking here
strangle me with them
cut them up twist them into rope hang me
you us the goddamn system

nothing should live
like this
furiously devouring
a whole world
everything beautiful.

*   *   *

The forest watches me as I go in
I know because I
answer to its answer

I am a stranger here
laid out along dead wood
and the timber whispers fire fire fire

but I burned a long long time ago
an ice age before another ice age

let my dread be a breath out
let leaves tremble and trees

eventually fall.

The dinghy in flames at the water's edge
ditchmoss and pondweed
oars withering in the shrub
fish traps drawn up on land like
dreams we've ceased to speak of
dead fish silent stink
black slime
boots smacking
out gone.

We are trees that fall from stillness
we are thickets burning and children

grown in the ashes we are rain we
balance on falling stars.

We are uprooted trees
ancient beasts that cling
to a future long lost to us
and rotting in a
wetland where words
are never language
holding our breath to listen
to the resistance eroding
grain by grain of sand
in the floodwaters
and the roar of the surge
that swaddles us
in forgetting.

I rest my paddle on the side
the stream meanders through
the watermeadow watches me in silence
like entering a churchyard
and the city grows quiet
lifted away by the dead
stone foundations buried in the landscape
you glide along the gravel paths
blackbird and robin
centuries-old ghosts
once here was a forest
one day you too will fall
and the living pass by whispering
with soft pulls of the paddle and sighs
long as rivers.

The city's sparkling windowpanes
and scents of backstreet greenery
mock-orange fresh-baked bread and
asphalt steaming summer
always a few words
and sentences
lost
among the cobblestones
along the pavement lost
sprawled in our seats at the sidewalk café
our laughs are vines
on dead trees
still finding the light
lapping it up.

Sights and whispers
from a forest in fall
and what once lived there
won't come back
as itself but
as something I won't know
remember the pygmy owl in the rowan tree
only one I ever saw
and eagle-owl short-eared owl northern hawk-owl
boreal owl Ural owl tawny owl
in that order
gone.

We are trees that fall from stillness
we are ashes in silt the creeping moss

gather our voices in urns
we are the memory of the forest

preserve us.

The river presses in
between the parking lots
smells of grease and char

the pedestrians are us
when we were on our way
somewhere else
in another state of mind

and we share the experience

afterwards we lie cool from swimming
at the open window

are met and enchanted
by time's blinding absence

while the deliveries rattle
through the morning hours.

We are abandoned farms
walls peeling

like faces in the desert
peering through the battered woodwork

came to us our loneliness
where grasses dance in the wind
despair grasping the broomstick

days dragged through rain
and distant music.

Steel gates steel rail steel storm drain
the city shook us out from its face

a dream of constant spring
of constant access connection

I heard the elevator descend
and come back up

the steel bars rattled
opened and closed

in my dream you rang the doorbell
I did not know it was my door

everything worked
lights on and off
up and down
water electricity

the flower bulbs in the churchyard
sprang out of the dark.

Deer flee owls fall from the sky
the blood burns the embers cool

we are trees that fall from stillness
sprawling bodies at rest at last.

Fall and I will lose it all
the forest lets me die and I will not
be missed

whooper swans sweep overhead
rowan berries ripen waxwings
fall in clusters round the farms
and outbuildings

can no longer find my way

out

gone.

Out on skis among snow-heavy pines
snow that slips from the branches
snow inside my collar snow on the
long marsh that can no longer see
all thaw all stream
time ceases to mean
after only a few days decades
rest and snow
slipping from the branches.

The patience of the winter trees drawn in chalk and coal
now the birches bend over the trail
the twigs cling with
fingertips
overdrawn with frost's
fleeting chill
the spirits rest
and you catch your breath
mid-shoveling
say you didn't know
say you chose to burn
say you are a forest
that lays itself down freely
to be taken
to the mill
say I can come with you.

* * * *

Those of us who know love speak of death
all the others speak of love

dig me a shallow grave
I want to feel the ground frost grip

and I want to feel the thaw
when the spring sun warms it.

I grasp at the TV images phrases
that eat my language and memories

morning news traffic jams
overtime rewards programs
all used up

the blackened photos in the backyard
and the kids' shows all
used up

grasp at the poems
but they have been used up

grasp at those starving
they pull me over the fence

grasp at the desperate
they hold me in their arms.

Mile after mile of
monotonous cellulose
woods without language
no words no fire

black liquor

traveled where you cannot follow
and farthest into the ravine
in darkness and glittering woodmoss
the fallen thousand-year pine
transformed into slow
flames.

Comfort that the birdsong overwhelms
comfort that thickets grow green

comfort that light rain
comfort that clear sky

comfort amidst concrete and brick
that forests rise from the ashes

that the flycatcher flies
that gulls magpies jackdaws

that woodpeckers chickadees life
takes back what it gave up.

Dragonflies hum like solar-powered
drones grain whitens in the wind

grieving what was never ours
grain spoiling in the cisterns

grieving what was never meant for us
the fields bear a memory of darkness

where none of us find footing anymore
generations of the sweat of our brow.

Comfort when the birch unfurls its
tender leaves when the pines hum

a concert of thousands
singing in rapture

comfort that life wells everywhere
comfort that it grows out of the dark

earth where death just now
grabbed and grabbed.

Grieve for those who don't come back
grieve the owlet the hawk in flight

grieve that the smallest perch

grieve for everything already
lost

grieve for our childhood
forests.

Comfort that life's unbending triumph
out in the parking lot

cracks in the chimney
boots and blue coveralls

where I am you cannot find me
scrapes in the red bogmoss
where the springwater swells

it is green without a care
to be green it grows
without a care to grow

we are the ashes after eskatos,
the silence does not belong to us.

THE STRETCHED NECKS OF STILLNESS

1. *Here are the climbing shadows of the dead*
lips and voices in flight
in the mouth of the living and
paths like winding
echoes and memories

2. *an invisible weave of questions and calls*
hearts stilled and
the wings hang,
the wellspring's mirror
trembles

3. *sings of the dead their*
wounds and songs
wet and heavy
leaves over the ground
steps on the paths of echo

4. *the mists' flying veils and*
gilded, blackspeckled
leaves tremble in the scrub,
here are their words
salvaged songs

5. *bare the beloved, the frightened,*
the fallen, the unseen's
vast longing's
breath probing
fall morning's

6. *wolf lichen, reindeer lichen, white*
branching lungtree like
soft and pulsating
gray and whitegleaming
fingers reaching through moss

7. *cup lichen, white lichen, wet tentacles*
tickle and scratch at the air
the flighty morning air
leaves resting
by frost corroded red

8. *cowberries watery*
bitter and speckled
lichens and mosses
with patterns like
venn diagrams

9. *built in stories*
starshaped mosses
brushes and bristles
bear moss, star moss
and other songs like

10. *soft blankets that cover*
the outcrops and climb
rocks and treestumps
pineleaves, blueberry, heather
that tousled and wet

11. *stand in drifts among stones*
gray and pale like withering
dead they stand in the mist
and sing in the wind's eye's
rough light and dirty

12. *breath, a smell that glides*
in the forest dulled,
a day like this dulled,
the sounds, movements, even
glances dulled

13. *between the trees, wary*
crooked contorted
trees the rowan
scrub, willow,
and clusters of birches straggling,

14. *their windless voices and tones*
of the dead, their
songs when they fly,
creeping up into our faces
flattened, monochrome,

15. *and fleeing, clutching at*
slick surfaces, clutching at
scents and voices in this
wheedling life that whispers
and rustles october mornings

16. *where the cold spring spouts*
from a rusted iron pipe struck down
by a hammer in unknown past
come here with song, with
voices with music brought forth

17. *in the pores of the earth,*
tentacles, senses scattered
and in the undergrowth, among
the trees, in the very air
attendant faces and

18. *traits, imagined and*
I see bodies move
when the lifting mist
when the droplets, when I
hear steps, hear falls, hear

19. *disharmonies drift and*
mingle, tasting the air, the tones
the swarming years, the
darkly and secretly developed
images, the melodies, the

20. *moving, in faces sown*
twitches
songs
  for the dead brought forth
  in this way watched

21. *and now brought forth*
witnessed
movements like a
morning with white fog
outside the bedroom window

22. *a clear mist*
transformed into pregnant
droplets on leaves and windows
let the gaze fall
and out there

23. *they move*
they want in
they seek you
and you answer
come, the day draws near

24. *we venture out into the land*
the flooded
drenched in mist
and damp, in cold and
wet winds draped

25. *drafty, cold and*
silent land,
the fall-still trees,
the scrubs, the whitened grass
with steps, rips, frost

26. *with movements from us*
from the mortal
to the already crossed
they who sing our songs
they who remember our lives

27. *they who cluster in the corners*
in our faces in our
bodies and how we move
the dancing and singing
they who pull us

28. *down*
they who suck us
down
    and want us
they who desire us

29. *whom we feel desired by*
they who sing us downward
down into the damp
into the moss and lichen
down into the scrub, the silent

30. *frozen*
reddened sprigs that tremble
on the paths
where we hurry on
where we hear voices

31. *where we rest in our bodies*
the movements of our bodies
the movements of the land
that sing us
the trees, bushes, grass

32. *the sprigs, moss, lichen*
their tattooed bodies
their would-be shadows
in an invisible weave
how we take them in

33. *devour them*
make them us
draw them down into our lungs
let them then be pumped
into our bodies

34. *in our movements*
in our movements' strength and sorrow
how we become them and how we
breathe them in and how we
are one another in the october air

35. *these cold mornings*
when the trees rest leaning in the air that
wet and heavy clasps the land, its
tones and values, its shifting
scents, salt, iron, moraine

36. *draw them up into the pipe*
where your cupped hands
fill, the silver running
over your hands, between, embraced
and cold running

37. *as little needles in the flesh*
little birds in the bush
singers that mint their coins
on stone slabs like bodies
filtered through centuries

38. *glacier-rolled ridges of stone*
and sand and like a tremor
everything surges out
and the body of space
the worlds that roll

39. *through bodies and centuries*
dancing in dawn light
in october rolling in and out
of bodies beaten and
aching between stretched

40. *necks and sheets that rest heavy*
and sweating under the window
under the draft of air
from the centuries out there
the october mist like

41. *wingbeats, tones from distant*
rapids, from dams,
hammers, axes, saws, and
other tools that
the dead handle

42. *when they press themselves in, into our*
rooms with their wounded hands cool,
cool us, cool our burning bodies
the aching joints, the fevered sores that bloom
on our limbs

43. *give us that water, the silverwater, the ironpipewater give us*
its body its out and in breathing, let us become
the purling, the prickling, the cold and fill your
hands with us drink us and fill us and see us
lie down here in the scrub, the lichen, the trembling

44. *tentacles on the outcrop, let us lie on the smooth rock*
and take in your steps as you seek
a bed of moss unknowing, these smells seeking
voices that speak to me, these sounds and smells that
fill me

45. *with life, with voice and life, with silver and cold, these*
bodies that enter me and are me and are the forest
and the breaths and are the sounds that rise from
me and the smells I emit and are the taste
of silver and iron in my mouth, a voice from the forest deep

46. *my body, a voice that plays*
over stems and roots
and sheds its longing
over the leaves' desire, my movement
a distance built into the strength

47. *to go outside a morning like this*
when the church bells ring
out over the parish
as a warning
as a guide

48. *a solace for those who wander*
in its sound you are a stream
the full chime
of courage to forge
ahead a day like this

49. *out on a morning like this*
when the songs of the dead
echo through the land
the still, redtrembling
land of berries

50. *land of moss*
and moor
where you have learned to bear
where you have learned to follow paths
between houses and outbuildings

51. *between outbuildings and nothing*
paths that seem to lead into nothing
but gather from out there
the roaming souls of the dead
between nothing and

52. *when you are here*
you're one of them and
when you listen
to my story
it's their words you hear

53. *and if you've ever been there*
if these words are your words
if these are voices from your body
from your steps and paths
if these are cabins from your life

54. *standing out there in the fog*
the mist-enveloped outbuildings
buildings in cranesbill and celandine
warped and leaning like
shadows in the mist that

55. *moves through, from far, the building itself that*
moves when you lean against its wall and
it's spring the sun is warm you remember
and you are your body then and the voice that drifts
through you is the dead's septic blistering

56. *sore and the memory that drinks you, every time*
against a leaning shed between village and nothing,
between paths that are suddenly gone and paths
that take you to roads that lie frost-heaving and
contorted in scorching forests dry with

57. *pollen and roaddust and when you sit there, it's your*
life they drink, when you squint at the sun and
their pipes strike down into your veins, with each breath
you feel your life drain into the land and become
you, the land takes you over and you are a mirage

58. *and you are preserved and you feel the sun in your face and*
it's october again, morning, night, it's night, someone
in the doorway glances at you and out of your ribcage
a wide iron pipe grows silently into the room and the
hastening voices are the voices of the dead

59. *glinting in the wellspring where we cup our hands under*
our breaths, our water, our land of harvests and
mines, of roads for us who wander
between villages and villages and villages
and nothing between us and us and nothing between

60. *nothing between what is empty and what is also*
empty we wander and you get in the car, you touch
the dashboard it's cold, the car is cold,
the october mist moving here this morning moves
around the car and your movements in the car and

61. *when you sit the seat is cold and when you touch*
the dashboard the plastic is cold and reminds you
of a friend, a close old friend that is no
longer, and you wonder what's moving
and you come to think of hair,

62. *cool yellow hair in the latewinter cold against a red wall*
and shone through by the spirit and with red fingertips
touched, breathed in, counted, exchanged, and made memory,
an echo and the key is turned in the ignition and it's a hand
and it creates her in you when you feel the cold like

63. *a cool and timid wondering hand, this loss in*
your fingertips, this morning with loss in the air,
every drop, every grass, each little movement in
gilt frightened vibrating or already fallen,
falling, already in flight, these redtinted

64. *blackspeckled sometimes trampled these small*
erring scraps of life that fall to the ground, through
churchcall and bronzetone, through your movements
when you get in the car and your fingers draw lines in
the mist on the windshield, key in the ignition, the dirt road

65. *that stretches scarred into prehistory, a wounded*
roebuck in a ditch, a pair of whitepointing fingers in mud, a
swerve a shout, what are we, sighs that flicker in different
windows and mist on the metal like stranded droplets and
windshield wipers like branches and leaves that stick,

66. *ride along, and the engine that revs it's a*
Saab and You are dead, feeling with fingers how the red wall
stains them and I dip them in all the dead and
taste it and it is fall,
and it is fall

67. *and the songs of the dead*
brought forth
a morning like this in october when
whales in the strait spout stacks of
arctic sea into the air, like pillars of soul and desire

68. *and you squint at the light*
the trees' branches tremble
a body comes toward us
a body of light
a body of sound and smell

69. *a body of pain at the temple after an unusually hard*
blow a body of heat in the throat after an unusual
effort a body comes toward us in our
apprehension, fear, our frightened eyes
that squint at the sun

70. *our blind spots where the warmth of our conversations*
lingers through night and sleep and finally
in this taste,
these bodies, in this
improbable meeting, lingers

71. *through weeks and waking nights*
lonely, empty, drifting skies
and shows you and memory
and it's you and I
and all the conversations that have ever

72. *been scattered out here in grasses and songs,*
conversations in purling iron pipes and winding
streams in rippling shadows in swampwoods,
shadows in outbuildings leaning between
paths that winding whisper between

73. *soil and nothing between*
conversations and echoes
their very own paths
little roads that ripple in the forest
dirt roads, before this paths

74. *before this fault lines*
before this calls
calls
like the bells' chime from their
birchbark throats

75. *and the heat*
of their throats
their hands
their warm touch
against your cold skin

76. *the warm breath that rises from the lake*
cold mornings, the warm smell from
dung heaps and their conversations
from the bodies of warm animals and
their conversations, how they bellow

77. *out of their birchbark throats*
how they hasten between the trees
how they are glimpsed and disappear,
change gears
roll up the window

78. *they aren't gone yet*
the engine is warm
the droplets on the hood vibrate and begin
to run, evaporating like cold smoke
and the grouse hen picking gravel

79. *the shine in her eye*
the radio starts
dragging itself through the fertile hour
drawing you out of your thoughts
while the blood still pulsates

80. *and the paths still gather*
branch out and disappear
appear and voices crystallize and
waves, surfaces made rough by conversations,
intentions of the dead's

81. *celebrated songs that open wounds,*
sharp edges in the eyes like
smoke from welding, I imagine an extension
I imagine that it's you and I and one of us
is missing and the other is missing somewhere else

82. *and you lean against a red timber wall*
that sheds its color and I see your hair and
you are here, taking a curve on the wrong side of the road
blinking, the steering wheel glides through your hands
the hard plastic grip, the fingers that glide

83. *through hair and plastic that glide through life and death*
the hard fingers that nip the grass that frostbitten
sails with the wind this way and the other and I follow
with my eyes the frostgrass swaying and the movement of
the sun at the horizon and think death, they think

84. *songs of passing conditions, rhythms, pulses, takes,*
distances to heed to blend to bestride
think all these sensations as though in a single song
as though in a glittering eye by the roadside
and that's why I know

85. *that everything takes place*
concerts
letters stacked into bibles
sounds traced to real things
real movement

86. *and I can say nothing else*
the songs are theirs, are yours
if you read me,
you read the dead
and their voices in me

87. *their climbing shadows*
and invisible weave, their expanses of light
as they've been given me, the words of the dead
sinking through me and you listen
rather than being the one to dance

88. *in humming fields of heather, lichen-blankets,*
rugs of pine rather than
sounding the horn in dulled october morning,
stepping aside, out of sight and
perception, stepping into the other,

89. *the others, you know what I mean*
you've been there
you've listened
and together
we write lakewater that lies motionless at dawn and

90. *meets colder air pouring down from*
the heights when night ends and the tone rises
the water runs back into its spring out of the ground
called back and brought back, to conversations in church
to flowerbeds, to the devastation

91. *where we rest in damp sheets*
stretched out, entwined and wet
squinting at the sun through the blinds
the light shining out there
through the mist

92. *a warm vapor in the garden*
embracing our shrubs
our ripening blackcurrants
our buried sorrows
and confessions

93. *and our longing, hand in hand*
with loss in all these million droplets
these million nerves that glimmer
in the dark, bones, luminous
little worms, synapses

94. *drawers half-open*
red
gaping
with rows of black teeth
we won't escape, you know that

95. *how buildings swallow us*
the air fills with their waves
vibrating, conversations covered
overlapping conditions
discontinued safety labels and

96. *regulations in several languages*
I see and I think and through all this you rise
a voice
lost and found again out there between the paths
that come and go between outbuildings and nothing

97. *your hair, your voice, your city*
buildings with rebar, risers,
electric grids and desks in room after room and you
lie in each one and in the dim light that
filters through the blinds and the dead

98. *and half-open drawers that gape,*
small hands tightly clenched, small warm frightened hands
under the covers in room after room and next-of-kin
ready with red wool blankets
but we have the voices already inside us

99. *and we have the dead's glances in the doorways*
and if you've come this far you can no longer
deny me, you are one of us,
and we are them and all these visions
grow between paths and places

100. *where the chime where the honeyflower teeters as the deer*
passes by and pauses, still, in the clearing
the old mill's bridge lies cracked in the grass,
the old stone wall
the stream that withdraws behind dark doors

101. *steps and the sound of steps that rests in moldering planks*
in stony ground in whitemoss on the outcrops
all these voices that watch us when we pass
and we can't stop ourselves from hearing
can't stop ourselves from being the ones who set traces

102. *and tongues in motion through place and time because in us*
grows what reveals itself and it wants words
wants us in its embrace, because we are its
breath and the thousand the million droplets that
swing in the morning cold on

103. *october days to frost and split worlds*
with ropes swinging, rocked into the woods
a sleep of pasture and rubber boots
a sleep of widebrimmed hats of sledgehammers that strike
iron pipes and let their tone sound over the marsh

104. *stop, sink into the ground and stratify in*
trunks and roots, in lichen, the grayfingered
straggling lichen inch by inch,
in the mosses, starshaped, lobed or tufted, in the
wet leaves that gleam and redtinted brown

105. *and blackspeckled sink into the tone, the moraine, the*
thin layer of poor soil in the pine heath, that
tone where earthworms and beetles and
woodlice and caterpillars and all the swarming
life between paths that bear back and forth, between

106. *mouths between glances and fingers dragged through*
hair, fingers that feel the wooden handle weighing down the
iron and the body opening up and how
I go through all this
rocked to sleep

107. *made aware*
preoccupied but sleeping
meeting
watching shadows and echoes in the doorway
someone who draws my harmonies out of the moss

108. *lulled by the song*
gray through the pines
and the groping fingers
I soon arrive
at the neighborhood

109. *the yellow duplexes*
the pale pink bungalows
the lawns, raked and yellowing
the waking houses
the floorplans of gaping drawers

110. *and though you're no longer here*
I hear you climbing inside the walls
and it's not you but you
come to greet me
and I take you with me

111. *but it's not you*
it's a cold morning
and at last I come
back and out here
and it's the sea bellowing in the forest and

112. *the rush of the arctic ocean pillars and*
it's the ancient sites
that lift us at last with their thousand-year-old voices,
the electric wires and their songs,
the parking lots like still

113. *damp, silent and glittering*
places as though between paths as though between
words and voices and nothing
and alone when I turn from the forest track
leave the uneven paths

114. *leave the shining pairs of eyes*
in morning glitter collapsed
when I shroud
and seek my way in
and the eyes burn out,

115. *the pines stretch their long necks toward a hazy*
morning sky that flickers in white and gold
and overwatered lawns that wet with dew and
tapwater lie half the morning feeding
blackbirds that with tails bobbing lean

116. *like drunk conductors over the orchestra pit where they*
listen rapt but with heads a little cocked
jocular as though to deceive the crawling segments down
there then suddenly snatch and pull and pull and
pull through the night, alone

117. *with their firebeaks that search the cinders,*
the sprinklers, the driveways and cars that
rest in heavy exhalation all through the dark side of day,
the cold side of year, october, the rust
eats through, uncertainty, long mornings with sleep and tea

118. *and coffeepots that shining in purple plastic with*
beaks of fire with cold black plastic that glides through
the fingers and the dashboard where a red lamp
shines for oil and engine trouble and old
yellow cars parked along the road and

119. *the middle clearly marked clearly shining middlewhite a kind*
of utopia a picture a kind of awareness in the asphalt a
clear thought that runs under the tires that glide in over
the asphalt road, the bigger one, Myckle Road where I biked
as a child and gathered impressions and scents and

120. *unexplained sounds and voices that flocked and*
swayed among cairns and paths in the forest, between
day and place, between my footworn fishing paths
and since-centuries trampled paths not yet
faded despite the absence of voices, of people, guided

121. *or footworn, the absence of voices gathered, archived*
and registered leaps, embraces, blueberries bursting between
your fingertips and how you desire and press juice
and seeds and delicate peel into a slim roll and the juice
like a thin trickle but still a clear

122. *image and how desire in this and the one who no longer*
exists but wakes you in this air, this speed,
these gaping drawers the walls gaping how what
you thought to say and never said, in the unsaid how
the gaping in itself encroaches on desire and settles

123. *like a damp and warm red blanket that pricks the eyes*
when they burst and the seeds trickle out like
a thin vein in the fingertip opened with a sharp knife and
bares your longing and regret at being among the dead
to see to hear to sing these songs yourself instead of

124. *being the one who writes and the one who wanders on paths*
between forest and places that, hollow and imprecise,
glide in the undergrowth and taunt and escape us,
our footfalls our feet our attempts to be there,
be what is revealed, what is me and you in this

125. *shifting, these dirt roads and the centerline glittering,*
the cold spring that spouts over whitemoss that red and
slimy from iron with purple streaks leaks
between grasses trembling in the water embraced
and moved and by the movement and its direction

126. *eager, to desire a movement that rooted in a red*
oozing wound, an open interpretation of pain how you
stare and try to give me your gaze a tremor over
your raised eyebrows though you are gone, really gone yet
sitting there when I come out

127. *of the house and approach the spring, its running water's*
murmur and arrhythmic clinking and it's dusk and you
are me and you sit there with your hand in the murmur
and trickle around your feet and the sedge grasses quiver
and how I suddenly see what you weren't, your

128. *song and our smelly dishcloths and the glittering*
snow and how you rise to your feet and your jeans
tight over your thighs and your red prickly sweater is
wet on the sleeve and you stretch your arm and
hand toward me and I feel how it

129. *smells of slime, of driveway, shine of eyes, cold plastic and*
the scalpel that opens a cut of moldering aspen leaves
with uneven edges that pale yellow and green, with
black stains that fall over your hair and your eyes
that close, your quivering eyelids and fear

130. *when the songs and voices as they've been given me and in*
this light that I know, really know it's you and
you're one of us and that it's not until now that a
future becomes real to me and a meaning
revealed and how we met and were bound to each other and

131. *what we said that it was no more than whispers,*
movements in the mist little glittering droplets in
the hair of dancing leafangels in morning's frostglittering
broadleaf trees what we claimed what we never dared touch
our fruits our secret and innermost voices that

132. *touched and brought forth in october haze and suburban*
morning tolled, parked with the handbrake and
firmly in first gear, see the blood spill onto
the seats and the radio shine green and the thermos settle
greenstriped on the floor in the back

133. *a bottle of disinfectant*
always ready, cotton
for the suddenly opened cuts
and scrapes, a room full of sleepers
forest tracks shining in morning fire

134. *glittering blue the snowground shines*
the mountaintops sail like terrible ships
shouts are heard, masts are climbed
little songbirds migrate infinite distances and
the pain in the right knee makes every step

135. *torture, hair by a wall, the kind of thing you remember*
while abstract concepts like distance and desire eat
a hole in the syntax and go unexplained, displaced and
unfinished, a shot through the thigh, a root canal,
I bend over the cold crystalseeing water and

136. *my fillings ache it's thursday, it's february, it's*
raining it's winter it's snowing it's autumn it's ice it's
snow over the infinitely distant firebeaks'
cinders and insights dig like nails into thighbone
and spine, like the absence of someone long since

137. *gone or newly left some quietly*
prescient shadow in the doorway when you go to bed
put your waterglass on the nightstand and
only in the corner of your eye
a gap in the blinds

138. *a dead tree out there,*
forest fires and resting texts,
stories gathered like morels in a basket
between paths that dissolve and their
directions in the scrub a throat black as coal and like

139. *heavy bronze bells, sings tones of lust and*
command in what you see when I see you in your eyes when
I see it created in voices of already gone, in chimes of
songs brought forth and sought, of throats and
openings in gold in fire openings like over

140. *miles-wide glitteropenings and quick cuts of silver and*
openings of cuts, of movements that cut
the eyes' movement of movements like markings in the road
against horizons far and near like a red timber sawmill
in the river by Myckle, where bootsteps and widebrimmed

141. *legends of pipes and iron that spouting out of*
the hospital bed and the gap in the blind like a cut
of red trickling and secretly gathered in baskets and
plastic bags packed with a dozen
graylings in the trunk and when I close the door,

142. *how the grouse's glitterstripes die how the mist and*
its movement die and desire begins to vibrate like
droplets and the glitter of an eye that button-black at
the edge of the road like an ache in the soul leering and
carefully leaning over the dark gap like a conductor over

143. *the segment of a story where the choreography is the*
most important, where unseen voices fool your inner eye so
plastic bits and stretching fingercuplichen in
the moss hide the obvious, the dead their
songs and the constant sensations of the living

144. *of cuts of bloodstream and knees that mile after*
mile already in lands where blocks of stone and
source and migrating birds' turns after
some damp breaths leave us but
this time for good, the bluethroat's heaving breast

145. *like an ocean with its starry eye in the dark and*
the voice a distant point that cuts through our
journeys wherever we are, however we find our way
or describe our movements on paths between hair
against red timber walls and

146. *nothing and outbuildings and the bluethroat's trembling song*
in the voice of your eye and your ear's constant
bleeding
this trickling of voices that
carries through your fingers,

147. *echoes in the vanishing paths of the scrub*
that straggle between eyes that glittering in
heather and fingers that press
the bluethroat's
body

148. *stretched neck and throat*
caught up with at last
and gathered,
preserved
in the songs of the dead and

149. *if you read*
you sing and
that's when your throat
and a wound that bleeds
in the half-open drawers of your friends' bedrooms

150. *and in the beds*
the hearts that beat and heave under
stargleaming oceanbreasts and it's theirs,
your friends, their wounds and songs
and the blankets they hold

151. *and it's your voice*
that is me,
your singing collection of bells
your newly awakened awareness in misty october morning
glitterstripes on the way home from work a late night when

152. *it's raining and the headlights sweep the road and*
the deer that's left its clearing and the honeyflower
in the storm of a sharp turn against time's trajectories
and you run out through the gap
and you run out over the wet flat leaves that

153. *redstreaked and blackened lie mouldering in*
songs and knees that mile after mile run on
their words their small hands outstretched trembling
with a dissolving red horizon like a breast like
outcrops smoothed by the ice age, where hooves scrape

154. *moss and water trickles and in the bay whales*
heave around and around only to swim straight onto
the shore and lie, their exhalations cutting
the music into rough pieces and you must lean ever
closer to hear

155. *and you stretch your wings*
and you pull and pull
and you return
constantly
to where you learned to bear

156. *to where the swans return white*
after their long winters
with their stretched necks
their sounds pressed out of throats
their clipped wings their

157. *broken necks and the red*
that bubbles from their beaks
their gurgling calls when they
return white and stained
white, with cutting wings

158. *the hum of their lungs when they breathe ten thousand*
feet up, when they roar from the higher atmospheres
break forth with their gurgling, forceful throats
the vertebrae broken, one by one crushed and how they
sing with what's left when they glide in over

159. *our land when they return to sheds and alder swamps*
and ponds with breadcrusts and rolls and snares
of piano string that sing their lost breath
and ours, we who watch
we who limp on our way

160. *between the trees*
and slip
and fall on the trigger
and wound the silence
and their cries for rescue

161. *and hear when we hear them*
in the cold flying skies
in the upturned eyes' dry
squinting, their songs when we hear
their eyepictures snap under

162. *our shoes and peer with rigid iris,*
and we travel, each our separate way and I ask myself
all this distance, all our movements,
our language
I see us act but I don't hear the dead when they

163. *whispering curse me at night*
I hear us, I hear the swans and I ask myself
our language when the finger on the trigger
the pen on the paper
when algebra and geometry and propositional logic

164. *in the ditch with its black eye in the*
flying skies' cold and dry calls,
the damp pondwater calls
the scream of fish called up from muddy depths,
we take them on,

165. *we lie down and listen to the ground and don't hear the*
world breathe, we hear empires march and not empires
long dead and rotting, an army
on foot and the sound of steps,
an army on horses most beautiful are

166. *their calls, of bodies*
their dry and cracking memory
their voices that creep
in the forests
in the mists

167. *in wellsprings at night*
and they want inside you and you listen,
their screeching wings when they glide only a few
feet above the plowed and steaming earth and
you don't hear their tongues dry in the room

168. *their tongues in the slime in the pondwater*
tight fists in small pockets,
dry burgerbuns in small hands
their songs, their cackling,
I lay down on the ground

169. *listen to*
open beaks
open wounds
their terror in the nets
in the steel wire snares

170. *their voices when they stretch,*
the voices of the white
the forgotten, untranslated
we are them
not their bodies

171. *not their hunger*
we are the broken leaves that rot on the water
we are the broken words in our own stomachs
we are what we hear or think we hear
and for that reason you keep reading, because you know

172. *and we're the ones who know*
you and I
and I'm coming now
don't be afraid
it's not the end

173. *it's not the beginning*
it's the white beats
under rainheavy skies
that drift back
and forth in the valleys

174. *between the overhanging mountains and*
the cold nutrient-poor lakes and
the fatty fish that wander between these seasons
and returning ice between these ages, their
steps and journeys and the return, the

175. *return itself on crooked wings*
with poles of peeled young pine
with skis of birch with secret
messages like tattooed bodies
buried in ancient libraries

176. *raised by echoes,*
swans in the swamp
with wings like sharp
tools, and their songs
build a tone to call us

177. *like insects build me when you read me build me*
build the tone build the gathering build the bowing
swans' broken necks and piercing eyes
broken stretches of wounds and scabs of pus of
boils and stresses and aching insides

178. *five swans stretched wide on our inner horizons*
with wings in wild struggles with air and illusions
with images as resistance that lift that force their way inside
us the constant beat in our bodies in our
bubbling blood a struggle over necessity,

179. *its different directions that settle in the body and are a*
force when astronomical events set their snares
and cotton balls with disinfectant on our internal bleedings
and our internal bleedings' thirsts and threads
that hold us in place and away from one another,

180. *from one another, a light fine and filtered*
in tissue and fluid brought forth
in the force and direction of our ears
in that we hear ourselves inward hear ourselves
spread out feathers in sections and assembled

181. *cut through creation and minute through*
your inner fires that bellow airborne devouring
voices, renewal, seeking the room
of rest of pause and silent safety and still
we only see, we only know

182. *the mist, the leaves, the bristle of mosses, pattern of stars*
in one another in me and in you and we are these voices
this running water and five swans that
bound tight drag their wings in red sinking skies
and in spite of this a gaze, a recollection and you turn

183. *and turn again and it's me and it's you*
and we turn and the swans rise to their feet
and beat their sails like ships they rise
and stretch across constellations their tongues their throats
their roars of jealousy of devotion and return here

184. *to the pondwater, the mist-enveloped land,*
the pine heaths and alder swamps and birchwoods,
how you grow still how you listen to their broken throats
when they call your name, when they return
and you listen to the writings of their wings when

185. *you see their beaks wide open and tongues how they*
work they circle the land and return
and their eyes shine and you step out onto
the porch and you call here they come and you want
someone to confirm your memory and your child and the

186. *movements in you that are the climbing shadows of the dead*
that you sing and hear the white wingbeats
that you cannot help but sing
their wounds and memory's

MATS SÖDERLUND was awarded the Swedish Writers' Union's prestigious Catapult Award for best literary debut in 1992, and has since received numerous literary awards and scholarships. He describes himself as "a forester from the north" with deep roots in Nordic folklore and the Northern narrative tradition. He has released eleven collections of poetry as well as works of fiction and nonfiction. Söderlund holds a Bachelor of Science in Social Work and served as Chairman of the Swedish Writers' Union between 2005 and 2012.

OLIVIA OLSEN is a writer, translator, and teacher based in Sweden. She holds a BA in Literary Translation and an MFA in Literary Arts from Brown University, where she taught fiction to undergraduates. Her translation from the Swedish of the poetry collection *Homullus Absconditus* by Magnus William-Olsson was published by O'Clock Press in 2015; her latest writing can be found in *Black Warrior Review*.

FORREST GANDER was born in the Mojave Desert, in Barstow, California, and grew up in Virginia. He spent significant years in San Francisco, Dolores Hidalgo (Mexico), Eureka Springs, and Providence. With the late poet C. D. Wright, he has a son, the artist Brecht Wright Gander. Forrest holds degrees in both Geology and English Literature. He lives now in Northern California with his wife, the artist Ashwini Bhat.